INTERNATIONAL ENVIRONMENTAL POLICY

BETWEEN CONTRADICTIONS AND EXPECTATIONS

Alexis KOMENAN

INTERNATIONAL ENVIRONMENTAL POLICY

BETWEEN CONTRADICTIONS AND EXPECTATIONS

INTRODUCTION

The environment has become an unavoidable subject on the international political scene. The situation of ecosystems, natural resources and the living environment is a matter of concern and calls for at least concerted action between the various States. The establishment of environmental issues as a global concern has taken the form of the gradual construction of a framework for consultation under the auspices of the United Nations. The motivation behind this policy framework is to define a human course of action in order to preserve the integrity of the planet and, consequently, the future of man on Earth.

While it is unanimously agreed that none of us can live in an unhealthy or hostile environment, other aspects of the issue are hotly debated at the international level. From the postulates of radical environmentalists to the arguments of supporters of the "American way of life", as well as the demands of environmental NGOs and the positions of emerging countries, the field is disputed.

In this analysis, we propose to comprehend the political evolution of the issue. From the traditional orientations taken by environmental governance at the international level, one has designed - or recalling - new solutions that are considered safe and sustainable for the planet, and therefore for mankind.

PART 1

THE CLASSIC ORIENTATIONS OF ENVIRONMENTAL GOVERNANCE

Social and environmental problems are the subject of individual or collective reflection by the actors of world political life. These reflections permit to guide the course of things in varying degrees, and to draw up a framework for the standardization of aims, choices and actions. Therefore it is important to be familiar with the traditional framework for environmental action, through international institutions and international civil society.

CHAPTER 1

THE INTERNATIONAL INSTITUTIONS

In response to progressive warnings about the first negative manifestations of economic models based on all-round production and mass consumption, the United Nations (UN) has given increasing attention to protecting the planet. As a result, a comprehensive legal framework has been developed and greater attention has been paid to the issues of global warming and pollution.

1. The Overall Legal Framework for Action

The United Nations system, based on the ashes of the Second World War, is composed of various consultation frameworks based on legal principles and designed to develop responses to various local and international political issues. While the post-war world had to respond to the socio-economic emergencies of the moment and the pressures of decolonization, environmental issues, on the other hand, only exceptionally came to the fore.[1]

However, awareness was raised, in particular with the conference on the environment organized by the United Nations in 1972, with the emergence of the concept of eco-development,[2] and especially through the famous Brundtland Report, produced by the World Commission on Environment and Development (UNCED), which popularized the concept of sustainable development.

This work has raised the alarm and brought the ecological theme to the forefront of the political arena. With the world symposium organized in 1977 by the United Nations Environment Programme (UNEP) on desertification,[3] the outlines are drawn for concrete actions at the State level: interconnection of social justice, economic development and environmental preservation.[4] Thus, the first protocols and conventions, dealing with regulating whaling (Washington, D.C., 1946), on wetlands of international importance, particularly as waterfowl habitats (Ramsar, 1971), on protecting the world's cultural and natural

---

[1] In particular, there was the International Convention on the Regulation of Whales in Washington, D.C., in 1946.

[2] Set of principles set out by Ignacy Sachs, author of the book *L'écodéveloppement: stratégies pour le XXIe siècle*, Collection Alternatives économiques, Paris, éditions Syros, 1997.

[3] United Nations Conference on Desertification. Nairobi, Kenya, 1977.

[4] These are the three pillars on which sustainable development is based, according to the Brundtland Report.

10

heritage (Paris, 1972), will be followed by many others: the Convention on International Trade in Endangered Species of Wild Fauna and Flora, CITES (Washington, D.C.), 1973); the Convention on the Conservation of Migratory Species of Wild Animals (Bonn, 1979); the United Nations Convention on the Law of the Sea (Montego Bay, 1982); the Protocol on the Reduction and Elimination of Surplus Chlorofluorocarbons (Montreal, 1987); the Conventions on Climate Change and Biodiversity and the Declarations on Environment and Development and on Forests, a series of texts resulting from the Earth Summit in Brazil (Rio de Janeiro, 1992); the Convention to Combat Desertification in Those Countries Experiencing Serious Drought and/or Desertification, particularly in Africa (Paris, 1994); the Kyoto Protocol in Japan, which was the outcome of the Third United Nations Conference on Climate Change (Kyoto, 1997). In 1995, the conference on climate change in Berlin and the conference on the protection of the ozone layer in Vienna were held. Others followed.[5]

At the regional level, regarding Africa, the African Charter on Human and Peoples' Rights, the legal basis of the former Organization of African Unity (OAU), adopted in Nairobi on June 28, 1981, "is the first international human rights

---

[5] These include the Copenhagen Conference (Denmark) on Climate Change (7-18 December 2009) and the Cancun Conference (Mexico) on the same subject (29 November-10 December 2010).

instrument to state clearly the right to an environment."[6] In the West African sub-region, initiatives such as the Coordination Commission for Parks and Reserves of the countries of the Conseil de l'Entente and the Tripartite Commission of Côte d'Ivoire, Guinea and Liberia for all the reserves of the Nimba Mountains are to be put at the disposal of the governments concerned.[7]

Two issues are particularly important: global warming and pollution.

2. The Issues of Global Warming and Pollution

One of the major themes discussed at international meetings is global warming.

The rise in global temperature, a source of worrying changes in natural terrestrial processes, and the deterioration of the stratospheric ozone layer, phenomena mainly attributed to human activities,[8] are the basis for a

---

[6] Abraham Gadji, "Droit de l'homme à l'environnement. Saisissez le tribunal en cas de dégradation de votre cadre de vie", in cahier *Économie & environnement*, p. VIII, Fraternité Matin, n° 12462, 22 May 2006.

[7] Francis Lauginie, *Conservation de la nature et aires protégées en Côte d'Ivoire*, CEDA/NEI Abidjan and Afrique Nature International, p. 395.

[8] Among other environmental impacts of human activities, the Intergovernmental Panel on Climate Change (IPCC) estimates, in its report published in 2007, the overall increase in GHGs between 1970 and 2004 due to these activities at 70%. Another demonstration of the study group talks

series of meetings, the most important of which was held in Kyoto, Japan, in 1997. This meeting resulted in the protocol's adoption of the same name. Following the 1992 Rio Framework Convention on Climate Change, it commits the international community to reducing its greenhouse gas (GHG) emissions by 5.2% by 2012. The ratification of this protocol is a sign of the willingness, at least of the decision of States to commit themselves to it. In the eleven years of its existence, 156 of the 192 States initially concerned had ratified the Protocol, including Côte d'Ivoire. Among these one hundred and fifty-six countries, there were twenty-two developed countries involved. Considered institutionally, the example of ecological awareness is beautiful. But politically, things have difficulties to start, since reductions in harmful gas emissions have remained insignificant, particularly for large industrialized countries that are also leaders in the world economy. With the United States of America in first position.

In order to boost the process, a Conference was held in Bali, Indonesia, from 3 to 15 December 2007. The aim was to prepare the follow-up to the Kyoto Protocol by drawing up a new agreement on GHG reduction, through the serious involvement of the world's major polluting countries, in

---

about "more than 90% chance", with regard to the role of man in global warming. The problem of the deterioration of the ozone layer was at the origin of the development of the Montreal Protocol (1987).

particular the United States, China, Australia and India. The other aim was to prepare a roadmap leading to a new climate agreement by the end of 2009. This consultation framework, the thirteenth of its kind organized by the United Nations on climate change, has caused major polluting countries to grind their teeth. Thus, "while it is undeniable that the door remains wide open to the possibility of bringing together the industrialized nations in two more years to discuss the reduction of greenhouse gas emissions, it remains equally true we have not curbed effectively all major polluters. With the United States in first position [...] And emerging countries such as India and China [...] on the way to becoming the biggest polluters, have hardly felt interested in quantified targets that have not been achieved. Rather, they were not prepared to admit measures that would hinder the momentum of their current economic expansion."[9]

Two years later, Copenhagen, the capital of Denmark, welcomed representatives of the entire international community to a historical gathering. The aim was to complete the discussions started at the Bali Conference by preparing a new "climate" roadmap for the post-2012 period, the expiry date of the Kyoto Protocol. From 7 to 18 December 2009, Copenhagen was the scene of fierce

---

[9] Moussa Touré, "Émission des GES. Des réductions encore insignifiantes", in *Fraternité Matin*, n° 13002, 13 March 2008, p. 3.

debates and negotiations between countries with an identical global interest, but whose immediate objectives are often out of step with each other. The Conference generated an agreement by which the parties intend, among other commitments, to limit global warming of temperatures to 2°C. But opinions were very divided on the consultation, which proved to be a "failure" for many disappointed participants and observers[10] - given the stakes - while others welcomed the humble but promising beginnings of a global climate policy.[11] Cap was then set for Paris in 2015, where all participants validated an ambitious aim of limiting the temperature increase to 1.5°C.

It should be noted that the very phenomenon of climate change is the subject of controversy sometimes mediatic. Opponents and the public often denounce, rightly or wrongly, the ideological underpinnings that would underlie the disclosure of one or the other theory.

Another sensitive environmental issue is the treatment of waste, which is a significant toxic load for the Earth. To address only one aspect, real waste piles have formed in

---

[10] Several developing states and environmental observers have criticized the bias and narrow scope of the Copenhagen Accord.
[11] This is the position of Ban-Ki-Moon, UN former Secretary-General, and Barack Obama, former President of the United States of America.

several ocean basins, such as the North Pacific or the North Atlantic.[12]

In the field of pollution, various conventions have been adopted to provide the basis for the overall framework for action on the classification, use, transport and management of waste. This is the subject of the Marpol Convention (1973) and the Basel Convention (1989). According to agro-economist Lester Brown, "an important step was taken in December 2000, when delegates from 122 countries met in Stockholm to approve an agreement banning 12 of the most toxic chemicals currently in use... Once 50 countries have ratified the treaty, which should take at least three years, implementation will begin."[13] Four years later, in May 2004, the Stockholm Convention on Persistent Organic Pollutants (POPs) entered into force.

Côte d'Ivoire is party to several environmental protocols and conventions at the global, continental and subregional levels. And the United Nations is showing, through the policy frameworks of UNEP, UNDP and the Clean Development Mechanism (CDM) under the Kyoto Protocol, that it has taken a significant step towards integrating environmental issues into its worldview. Civil

---

[12] Audrey Garric, "Le 7e continent de plastique: ces tourbillons de déchets dans les océans", in *Le Monde*, 9 May 2012.
[13] Lester R. Brown, *Eco-Economy: Building an Economy for the Earth*, W. W. Norton & Company, 2001, quoted from the French version, p. 201.

society actors around the world will have been their decisive levers.

CHAPTER 2

THE INTERNATIONAL CIVIL SOCIETY

Here it will hardly be a question of studying the emergence of an international civil society. Since humanity is interpenetrating and planetizing,[14] the subjects that interest it are also becoming more and more global.

This is the case for the environment. As Professor Philippe Saint-Marc says, "Space is one. Pollution knows no borders."[15] That said, it is important to review the history of the ecological awakening and to take an interest in the currents of this civil society in their conception of an environmental policy that would be a factor in sustainable development.

---

[14] Present participle of the verb "planétiser", of the expression "planétisation", neologisms used by Father Pierre Teilhard de Chardin, in *L'Avenir de l'Homme*, éditions du Seuil, 1959.
[15] Philippe Saint-Marc, "Protection de la nature", in *Encyclopædia Universalis*, 1982, vol. 13, p. 690.

1. The Ecological Awakening

In the political dynamics, the powers of governments and populations interpenetrate, in varying degrees, and according to each other's culture and political vision. A well-educated population, well aware of its problems and possessing an ideal of life, through its elites and mass movements, influences the decision-making process and political orientation of society. Thus, as simple as it may seem, governments have often been awakened to ecological awareness by elites and social, national or transnational groups.

For the rise of environmental concerns and their connection to human well-being are to a large extent linked to the work of millions of people thinking and working, within multiple organizations, in contact with the daily realities of an existence to be perfected.

The crucial nature of a responsible environmental policy came under critical point with the announcement by scientists in May 1985 of the discovery of a hole in the stratospheric ozone layer over Antarctica. This worrying discovery, as well as several setbacks such as the Chernobyl nuclear accident in the former Soviet Union and the pollution caused by the *Amoco Cadiz* ship in France, have put the entire international community on alert. Studies, reports and conferences are multiplying in all environmental fields. Men and women, social groups, research centers and institutes have been distinguished in information and action.

One of the first organizations to bring the message to the attention of the world was the Club of Rome, through its various studies, including the Meadows Report published in 1972.[16] In 1971, *The Entropy Law and the Economic Process* was published in the United States. Its author, Nicholas Georgescu-Roegen, already distinguished himself in the community of economists by arguing that the human economy cannot claim to be free from its fundamentally biophysical origin. Since 1984, the Worldwatch Institute, an American organization founded by Lester R. Brown, one pioneer in environmental and sustainable development research, has published *The State of the World* annually. Brown's ideas, an agro-economist by trade, initiator of the concept of eco-economy can be summarized as follows:

"Building an eco-economy is an exciting and rewarding project. It implies that we can live in a world where energy comes from wind turbines and not from thermal power plants, where recycling industries replace extractive industries, where cities are designed for people, not for

---

[16] Donella Meadows et al., *The Limits to Growth*, 1972.

cars... The construction of an eco-economy will affect every aspect of our lives. It will change the way we light our homes, what we eat, where we live, how we use our leisure time... It will offer us a world in which we will be part of nature, instead of remaining strangers to it." [17]

Lester Brown and his team have a strong influence in environmental and eco-political circles. The "Grenelle de l'environnement" in France testifies to the consideration of his analyzes around the world.[18]

Another prophet of a development adapted to ecological realities is René Dumont. He will have devoted much time to the problems of the Third World in general and Africa in particular. In his book *Démocratie pour l'Afrique*, he raises the environmental problem as one of the major issues facing the black continent - supported by its Western partners. René Dumont enshrined the entry of the environmental movement into political debate by running as a candidate in the 1974 presidential elections in France.[19] There is an emergence of "green" parties, particularly in Europe, and

[17] Lester R. Brown, *op. cit.*

[18] Jean-Louis Borloo, former French Minister of Ecology, Sustainable Development and Planning, cites Lester R. Brown as one source of inspiration for the work of the Grenelle de l'Environnement. Interview on 10 October 2007 in the Radio France International (RFI) programme "7/10" (source: Wikipedia, article "Lester Brown").

[19] He made his mark on the audience by presenting himself with a glass of water as a symbol of his argument.

the gradual creation of ministerial departments dedicated to the environment. A whole range of private institutions work with public partners and other social actors on the anchoring points in environment and development policies, thus making their voices heard in various international fora: the Institute of Economic and Social Studies for Sustainable Decline; the Observatoire de l'écopolitique internationale, based in Quebec (Canada); the Institut de recherche et de développement (formerly ORSTOM); the World Resources Institute in Washington; and the Wuppertal Institute in Germany.

Thus, as the ecologist movement develops, the various currents at work within it are emerging.

2. The Environmentalist Currents

Faced with governments and private actors who, having a weak or diffuse vision of the impact of their activity on the vital cycle of areas, often find it difficult to abandon the old economic model born of the Industrial Revolution, conservation and promotion organizations of nature and the living environment are striving to gain substantial resources to close this gap and influence the course of events. Little listened to at first because of the inevitability of local or transnational power relations and the immature interests of both sides, they end up integrating, particularly in industrialized countries, into the ambient political dynamics and, through awareness-raising, questioning and pressure, becoming necessary partners for public and private actors for the balancing of a socio-political system oriented towards the most mature social project possible. Real public policies are thus developed within the framework of environmental protection and the consideration of social needs by these structures, whose annual funding, averaging between $50 million and $100 million for a given organization,[20] comes essentially from private donations and also from subscriptions and membership fees, all united in this for a responsible ideal. These include the World Wildlife Fund for Nature (WWF), Green Cross International, The Nature Conservancy, Greenpeace and others. Other associations testify to the evolution of mentalities in favor of development based on economic ethics. Such as the Novethic center, corporate social responsibility and ethical investment, based in France.

The African continent has not remained on the sidelines of this numerical and political progress of NGOs, particularly environmental NGOs, even if the state of political culture and power relations are more delicate. Yet Africa, in search of well-being, lends itself as a breeding ground for reflection and action on the best paths to development. One

---

[20] Edward O. Wilson, *The Future of Life*, éditions du Seuil, 2003, quoted from the French version, p. 214.

of the best known "green" non-governmental organizations is the Green Belt Movement, founded by Wangari Maathai in Kenya. Because this woman, a role model for all those concerned with the well-being of nature and men, "regularly challenges corrupt political leaders, she has often been beaten and threatened."[21] Afrique Nature International works for nature conservation on a continental scale. Francis Lauginie, former president and founder of the Ivorian section of this NGO, publishes, in partnership with Ivorian conservation structures, a remarkable book entitled *Conservation de la nature et aires protégées en Côte d'Ivoire*. This 668-page book, published in 2007, is a major study available to people concerned about the country's real development.

Is it tantamount, in speaking of an international civil society engaged in environmental policies that benefit all - Humanity and Nature - to limiting its qualification to NGOs and those who stand out from it? No, because this would unfortunately ignore that the other actors mentioned in parallel with NGOs in the previous pages, from large industrial groups to the media and individuals with decisive action, have taken ecological concerns into account. Much remains to be done, we must acknowledge, but the first attempts are commendable to say the least. However, there

---

[21] Lester R. Brown, *op. cit.*

is a fundamental domain that is a key to the success of environmental advocacy: *environmental ethics*, which springs from the depths of man, from his philosophical and spiritual relationship with nature, with other living beings and with his environment. And it is precisely a fact that these forces are becoming increasingly involved. We find "Mother Nature" or "Mother Earth" to defend and preserve, "God's Creation" to promote. The importance of this paradigm is such that it undoubtedly makes up the cornerstone of the salutary process in which humanity must engage.

These various consultation frameworks reflect the spirit in which governments, at least the most enlightened and voluntary among them, aspire to commit themselves to the well-being of the planet, which is inseparable from the well-being of populations. The pattern of international environmental policy action, although somewhat narrow, is gradually being sketched out: protection and promotion of water, soil, climate, living species and mankind; responsible and management of existing energy resources and waste; and, above all, *progress towards a sustainable development policy*.

PART 2

THE NEW PARADIGM OF THE
ECOLOGICAL ECONOMY

Earlier, we discussed the indicators and standards that would form the basis of an environmental policy in which both humanity and the Earth would benefit, in contrast to the current situation. This environmental governance must of course take into account the needs of the economy, which is the essential foundation of human life. One detail, however, is that the economy we are talking about is in harmony with the ecological principles of the planet. It has been applied in the models of "bio-economy", "ecological economy" or "eco-economy" and developed by authors such as Nicholas Georgescu-Roegen, Herman Daly and Lester Brown.[22]

Forging an ecologically viable economy, as a corollary of a well thought-out environmental policy, means restoring the primacy of ecology over economics and imitating the cycle of Nature in our behavior.

---

[22] There are differences between the supporters of this current which, however, do not hide the unanimity established on an urgent need: that of reintegrating the human economy in harmony with the ecological dynamics of the Earth.

CHAPTER 1

THE PRIMACY OF ECOLOGY OVER ECONOMICS

The primacy of ecology over economics is both the obvious necessity and the great opportunity for real development of human populations.

1. The Obvious Need

We mentioned that many studies carried out by various national, international or non-governmental organizations competent in environmental matters show a rather swollen face of the Earth. These include those of the Food and Agriculture Organization of the United Nations (FAO), which estimates that about 13 million hectares of forest are disappearing each year worldwide;[23] UNEP, which notes increasing ocean acidification;[24] and WWF, which

---

[23] *Fraternité Matin*, n° 13002, 13 March 2008, p. 1.

[24] UNEP, *Annual Report 2008*. In 2014, a report on the effects of ocean acidification on marine biology confirms that acidification has increased by an average of 26% since pre-industrial times (Dorothée Laperche, "Changement climatique: l'acidification des océans s'accélère", in *Actu-Environnement*, 8 October 2014, URL address: https://www.actu-

estimates humanity's ecological footprint at a level exceeding 30% of the planet's regenerative capacity. The same report also points out that some 50 States are facing moderate or severe water stress.[25]

However, the various reports, while providing a worrying overview of the situation, also note and welcome the efforts made to change and improve the situation.[26] And faced with the anger of the earthly mother, our humanity, somewhat ashamed to discover its nakedness after many decades of *ego-economic carnival,*[27] can only negotiate, if not submit - more or less slowly - to the laws of its genitor.

In more concrete terms, this means that the current poor international ecological status, the consequences of which on human populations are already too measurable, requires *a change in the political and economic paradigm*: the primacy of ecology over economics. It is possible to

environnement.com/ae/news/changement-climatique-acidification-oceans-22917.php4).

[25] WWF, *Living Planet Report 2008*. According to the NGO WaterAid, more than 60% of humanity already lives in water-stressed areas (*The Water Gap– The State of the World's Water*, 2018, p. 2).

[26] For example, the implementation of the Montreal Protocol has had a positive impact on the situation of the stratospheric ozone layer, which, according to a UN report, is expected to evolve positively by the middle of the century. In its 2018 report on the state of the world's forests, FAO estimates that "the pace of loss has slowed in recent years" (p. xi).

[27] We understand by "ego-economic carnival" the sped up material growth of humanity achieved in ignorance and to the detriment of nature, then naively considered inexhaustible.

measure the political implications of such a conception by using the words of Professor Saint-Marc:

"It is the conception of the 'progress' that must be challenged; nature must no longer be sacrificed to economic growth and its protection must cease to be a minor concern to become the fundamental aim of humanity [...] The safeguarding of nature implies political action: not only with the State but also on the State, and by the most democratic means, universal suffrage." [28]

The primacy of ecology over economics is foremost an evidence. Ecology is the science of living environments and the exchanges that take place there. Economics is the science of producing and managing man-made wealth. However, is it necessary to stress that the production of wealth, not only does not take place ex nihilo, but also - in the phase where it interests current scientific and economic models - only takes place at a very marked stage in human life, *even though it has been produced and matured by the surrounding natural environment?*

The primacy of ecology over economics is then a necessity. Knowledge of the physical realities of nature and its functioning must determine human action to enhance this nature. We can never repeat it enough, ecological laws are

---

[28] Philippe Saint-Marc (with P. Antoine), *op. cit.*, p. 689.

naturally self-imposed and suffer none dispute without damage to life. Therefore, knowing how natural systems work and acting with respect for them is the foundation of any well-thought-out development. However, multiple proofs of the obsolescence of industrial development based on fossil energy and supported by a rapid urbanization and population growth in the so-called Third World States have been provided. And René Dumont added: "Like the oppression of women and the demographic explosion, *environmental degradation is a political problem:* it has even become the first, and it must be addressed *on a global scale.*"[29] He says further on:

"It is out of the question to generalize the Western way of life throughout the world: the energy and mineral resources at our disposal would not be enough... Let us detail our hypothesis: 1 or 2 cars gained by each African family (80 million families to date, 100 million tomorrow; let us add the 600 million Asian families - this last figure will be exceeded in the year 2000). I have already calculated that, if each of the cars in Asia required the same concrete surface area (garages, car parks, motorways...) as in California, there would be little agricultural space left available in most of China, Java, Indochina and the Indian subcontinent... In this absurd but suggestive hypothesis, the

---

[29] René Dumont, *Démocratie pour l'Afrique*, éditions du Seuil, 1991, p. 80.

known (and yet to be discovered) oil reserves would quickly be exhausted... " [30]

The primacy of ecology over economics is therefore a necessity, and not to recognize intellectually and politically this evidence is to walk blindly and thus get into a lot of trouble, whether in the short, medium or long term. The problem also arises for Côte d'Ivoire and it is about giving local examples as food for thought.

In an article in *Fraternité Matin* newspaper mentioning several violations of protected areas, Dr. Mathieu Egnankou Wadja, president of the NGO SOS Forêt, said "nothing more concrete is being decided on forest protection in Éburnie...[31] It is a real ecological crisis that awaits Côte d'Ivoire after the socio-political crisis we are experiencing."[32] Among the warning signs of this crisis, the president of SOS Forêt noted: the intensive and increasing sunshine, particularly noticeable in Abidjan, rainfall disturbances, respiratory diseases, skin diseases and other ailments, which are on the rise.[33] Almost a decade later, the

---

[30] *Ibid.*

[31] Neologism derived from the Latin noun "ebur", which means "ivory." It is used to designate Côte d'Ivoire.

[32] Moussa Touré, "Protection de la biodiversité. Une crise écologique guette la Côte d'Ivoire", in Cahier *Économie & environnement*, n° 97, p. VIII, *Fraternité Matin*, 15 May 2006.

[33] *Ibid.*

situation has not yet really improved.[34] In addition, regarding climate change, impact studies carried out by the Ministry of Environment, Water and Forestry in 2001 produced results important to consider: at the level of coastal resources, taking into account that sea level rise will be one metre, "54 km^2 of land will be flooded. Putting at risk the 4 million people living on the Ivorian coast, and the economic infrastructure there... A large part of the palm oil, rubber, pineapple, plantain and coconut plantations will be washed away. Especially the large oil palm farms producing 580,000 tons and coconut from which 37,000 tons can be extracted in the Abidjan regions. The roads will not be immune to these perverse effects of climate change: it is estimated that all the asphalt roads, tracks and bridges in the Abidjan region will disappear at 1000 km, with a rise of 0.5 m in sea level... The National Bureau of Technical Studies and Development, estimates that the total losses caused by the consequences of climate change on the Ivorian coast will amount to CFA francs 2355 billion."[35] And Lucien Djaha, National Coordinator of the Greenhouse Gas Inventory Project to reveal:

---

[34] See Martial Niangoran, « Changements climatiques à Korhogo. Protéger les bois sacrés en encourageant le reboisement », in *Fraternité Matin*, cahier *Environnement & développement durable*, 14 February 2013, p.20-21; Moussa Touré, "Protection des écosystèmes. Ces menaces qui pèsent sur la biodiversité ivoirienne", in *Fraternité Matin*, cahier *Environnement & développement durable*, 4 December 2014, p.19-20.

[35] *Fraternité Matin*, n° 13002, 13 March 2008, p. 3.

"About 3.5 million people will have to be displaced, abandoning major investments such as factories, housing infrastructure, administrative buildings and others, which will have to be rebuilt. This will require enormous financial resources from the public authorities."[36]

Thus, designing political actions based on the environmental situation will only be of the greatest benefit to leaders and other social actors.

2. The Great Opportunity

The primacy of ecology over economics is an opportunity. It is no exaggeration to say the world is at a crossroads at the beginning of the 21st century. What assessment can be made? The global political system, dominated by the market economy and technology, has revolutionized human life considerably. It had and has its advantages. But also its disadvantages. Like any human work, we will say. But why then insist on the disadvantages? Because the delicate state of the situation requires it. For example, we discussed earlier the *2008 WWF Living Planet Report*. This organization estimates that at the rate of its current consumption, humanity will need two planets in the early 2030s to meet its needs. UNEP noted, among other

---

[36] *Ibid.*

degradations, an acidification of the important marine ecosystem in its 2008 report. And the International Food Policy Research Institute, based in Washington, to forewarn, regarding the black continent:

"The decrease in soil nutrients leads to stagnation or decline in agricultural production in several African countries. Unless African governments, with the support of the international community, undertake to find solutions to the problem of soil depletion, the decline in agricultural productivity will seriously jeopardize the foundations of sustainable economic growth in Africa." [37]

This suffices to conclude that the overall orientation and functioning of the global political-economic system shows unsustainable limits and that they need reform. For a long time, we based life on "the economy" instead of the opposite. We therefore need a turnaround. It is therefore encouraging to see a redefinition - albeit a laborious one - of economic policies from an ecological perspective in some States, most of them industrialized. If the eco-economic paradigm is - and must be - seriously taken into account by governments and major financial groups, this will lead to a huge restructuring of the economy as all

---

[37] International Food Policy Research Institute, *Nutrient Depletion in the Agricultural Soils of Africa*, 1999, in John Madeley, *Hungry for Trade. How the Poor Pay for Free Trade*, Londres, Zed Books, David Philip, coll. "Global Issues", 2000. Quoted from the French version, p. 54.

aspects of our lives are rethought taking into account our ecological relationship with nature. And as already noted, new modes of wealth production will emerge with their industries, their jobs, their workers. The ecologically based economy, which generates new and expanding jobs and educates human lifestyles, will then be a factor in an all too significant improvement in the quality of life and a royal path to social justice. This is a great opportunity for the States of the world in search of benchmarks, especially the poorest, to consider seriously their integration into a world where ecology will finally regain its rights. Where it will be necessary to relearn how to imitate the cycle of Nature.

CHAPTER 2

THE IMITATION OF THE CYCLE OF NATURE

The practical modalities of this vast system, which both originates from and determines environmental policy, consist in a political imitation of nature's own economy. Therefore, it is important to know some basic ecological principles and examples of ecological lifestyles for a successful integration of the current human economic system.

1. Some Ecological Principles

Nicholas Georgescu-Roegen was one of the first to demonstrate the basic importance of the environment for the economy, which must be integrated into biophysical dynamics for its sustainability. To do this, he establishes, based on the physical principle of entropy, that the economic process only transforms natural resources of low entropy (little or no wear) into products of high entropy (increasingly worn).[38] So he continues:

"In reality, the economical use of the low entropy land stock [...] is the main problem for the fate of the human species. To illustrate this, suppose that S represents the current stock of low land entropy and r a certain average annual amount of depletion. If we ignore the slow degradation of S, as we can do without inconvenience here, the maximum theoretical number of years required for the complete depletion of this stock will be S/r. This will also be the number of years at the end of which the industrial phase of humanity's evolution will necessarily end. Given the fantastic disproportion between S and the solar energy flux that reaches the globe each year, there is no doubt that, even with a very sparing use of S, the industrial phase of human evolution will end long before the sun stops shining. It is difficult to speculate what will happen then [...] Nevertheless, it remains certain that the higher the degree of economic development, the greater the annual

---

[38] Entropy is the second principle of thermodynamics in physics. Entropy is a "measure of disorder" (Georgescu-Roegen), i.e. a "function defining the state of disorder of a system, increasing when it evolves towards another state of increased disorder" and "the degradation of energy linked to an increase in this entropy. " (*Le Grand Robert*, 2005).

exhaustion r *will be and therefore the shorter the life expectancy of the human species.* "[39]

Lester Brown evokes some major mechanisms of ecological dynamics and natural economy of our planet in the following development:

"Ecologists understand the ecological processes that sustain life on Earth... They know that Earth's ecosystems provide services as well as goods, and that the former are often more valuable than the latter... Nature too is based on balances. These are the balances between soil erosion and new soil formation, between carbon emissions and carbon sequestration, between tree death and tree regeneration.

Nature depends on cycles to sustain life. In nature, there is no linear flow, no situation where raw materials enter at one end and waste leaves at the other. In nature, what one organism rejects is another's livelihood. Nutrients are continuously recycled. This system works. Our challenge is to imitate it in the economy's design.

Ecologists appreciate the role of photosynthesis, the process by which plants convert solar energy into biochemical energy that supports life on Earth. Anything

---

[39] Nicholas Georgescu-Roegen, *The Entropy Law and the Economic Process*, quoted from the French version, p. 55.

41

that reduces the product of photosynthesis, such as desertification, asphalting productive land or acidification of lakes by acid rain, reduces land productivity in the most fundamental sense." [40]

The author subsequently notes that states have unfortunately "expanded economic activity at the expense of sustainable yield and the fragile balances of nature." This situation persists despite the sum of scientific research undertaken and publications recorded, despite the sum of knowledge acquired on the functioning of the planet, despite the example set by certain communities and peoples who, possessing a certain ethics of nature coupled with high value environmental knowledge, use it for their greater good and that of their ecosystem.

2. Some Ecological Cultures

We will focus on the ecological practices used by the Bishnoi, the Essenes, known to others and rediscovered.

The Bishnoi are a people of India living in the country's north, especially in the state of Rajasthan. They have made themselves famous for their very radical sense of respect for nature and for all creatures. Thus, their ethics give rise

---

[40] Lester R. Brown, *op. cit.*, p. 124-125.

to a characteristic attitude towards the environment. For 500 years, the Bishnoi, who live on the edge of the desert, "have felled no trees or killed any animals. They even take care to filter the cooking water so as not to kill any small insects. Thanks to their way of life, the Bishnoi have been able to preserve a small lake and fertile land despite living in a rather desert region..." [41]

The Essenes, a term well known in theologiacal and archaeological circles, are a community whose origins date back to the beginning of humanity, according to its members. But the term "Essene" is best known for Proto-Christians and early Christians from the second century BC to the first century AD in Palestine, Syria and Egypt. Generally perceived by the scientific community as the authors of the Dead Sea Scrolls, many studies on them have been carried out around the world and research is ongoing. Like the Bishnoi, the Essenes have an original relationship with the environment. A modern Essene community presents it as follows:

"The Essenes are not believers, but practitioners. They have always gathered in villages to live according to their culture and with respect for Mother Earth.

---

[41] Renato Pichler, "Les Bishnoïs, une vie sans tuer", in *Vegi-Info*, April 2000.

Today, the Essene Villages are not parks to preserve a wild nature but living places in which man learns to live in harmony, in dialogue with the Mother.

It's a new way of being in the world. It is an ambitious project, a grandiose achievement." [42]

A little further on it is said the Essene villages are spaces "where all the kingdoms of nature are taken into account."[43] In Catholic Christianity, some monasteries still keep this way of life inherited from the early Church.[44] Such designs, based on a high knowledge of ecological principles, are as old as the community itself, according to the work of some experts. One of them, Edmond Bordeaux-Székely, a specialist in ancient texts attributed to Essenism, has written many books on the Essenes and has himself applied their proven ecological principles.[45] Here is what he says about humanity's environmental impasse in one of his books:

"Obsessed with an evil spirit of greed and competition, our society is devastating and foolishly wasting the precious capital of the planet's natural resources to produce an

---

[42] Essene website: etre-essenien.blogspot.com.

[43] *Ibid*.

[44] See the tradition of the Desert Fathers, of the Benedictine monks and of the Mount Athos monks, among others.

[45] Dr. Bordeaux-Székely is the founder of the Rancho Puerta Centre in Mexico. The ecological way of life of the Essenes is practiced there.

endless tide of useless, non-biodegradable and non-recyclable consumer goods.

Thus, an ever-increasing pollution of the sources of life on earth - atmosphere, oceans, rivers, lakes, soils, fields, forests - is developing at a dizzying rate, forever destroying thousands and thousands of life forms created millions of years ago. In the very near future, the centralized giant industry, this insatiable monster, will have completely separated us from the nature that covers our mother earth and will finish us by immolating our weakened, anemic and sick bodies at the top of a mountain of poisonous waste as big as the planet." [46]

The author also describes the Christian-Essene way of eating, housing, agricultural techniques and ecological concepts.

These ways of exploiting the land according to an environmental ethics, this ecological and emotional relationship with nature perceived as a mother and a nurse to love, respect and nurture are gradually being rediscovered by many in a generalized environmental crisis. This is especially true in an area such as agriculture. For example, John Madeley states that "many farmers are successful in improving and sustaining their yields through

---

[46] Edmond Bordeaux-Székely, *The Essene Way: Biogenic Living*, I.B.S Intl., 1981, quoted by Dr. Christian T. Schaller in "Santé Globale", his website.

methods based on proven agro-ecological principles that emphasize diversity, synergy, recycling and integrated management, community participation and strengthening. As a result, not only are harvests increasing, but biodiversity is being preserved and soil fertility restored."[47] He says "countries that have made significant strides in food security have done so largely by turning to appropriate and low-cost technologies. In Mali and Burkina Faso, for example, the widespread application of new water harvesting techniques allows farmers to better benefit from rainwater [....] The challenge of sustainable agriculture, says Jules Pretty, is to "maximize the use of local renewable resources". Pretty highlights the impressive increase in agricultural yields associated with this approach to agriculture."[48] Also, for example, "about 45,000 farmers in Guatemala and Honduras have increased their maize production so much that it has encouraged many people who have moved from the city to return to the countryside."[49] Other eloquent experiences of ecological agricultural techniques and environmentally friendly systems[50] show the need for integrating human activities into the ecodynamics of nature.

---

[47] John Madeley, *Hungry for Trade, op. cit.*, from the French version, p. 204.
[48] *Ibid*, p. 204-205.
[49] *Ibid*, p. 206.
[50] One example is the concept of "permaculture." It is an approach whose name rhymes with that of Bill Mollison, an Australian agronomist and ecologist, who says it is "based on respect for the land and people." The term

means "permanent agriculture." Proponents of this method rarely use any external inputs, but this does not prevent them from achieving high yields compared to users of chemical inputs. See John Madeley, *op. cit.*

CONCLUSION

International political action on the environment is driven
by an awareness of environmental issues, which often have
transnational or global implications. The common will of
governments, supported by the activism of some civil
society organizations, has led to the gradual construction of
a legal and institutional framework in this area. While
everyone agrees on the essential point, namely to preserve
the Earth, there is still a divergence of views and even
interests on the practical line to be taken in the management
of the planet's natural resources. Although changes are
generally slow and partial, it is still encouraging to see a
revival of ecologism at the global and local levels.

BIBLIOGRAPHY

BROWN, Lester, *Eco-Economy: Building an Economy for the Earth*, W. W. Norton & Company, 2001.

WORLD COMMISSION ON ENVIRONMENT AND DEVELOPMENT, *Our Common Future*, Oxford University Press, 1987.

DUMONT, René, *Démocratie pour l'Afrique*, Paris, éditions du Seuil, 1991 (with Charlotte PAQUET).

GADJI, Abraham, « Droit de l'homme à l'environnement. Saisissez le tribunal en cas de dégradation de votre cadre de vie », cahier *Économie & environnement*, p. VIII, in *Fraternité Matin*, n° 12462, 22 May 2006.

GEORGESCU-ROEGEN, Nicholas, *The Entropy Law and the Economic Process*, Cambridge, Massachussets, Harvard University Press, 1971.

INTERGOVERNMENTAL PANEL ON CLIMATE CHANGE, *Climate Change 2007: The Physical Science Basis*, IPCC, 2007.

LAUGINIE, Francis, *Conservation de la nature et aires protégées en Côte d'Ivoire*, Abidjan, éditions CEDA/NEI et Afrique Nature International, 2007.

MADELEY, John, *Hungry for Trade: How the Poor Pay for Free Trade*, Londres, Zed Books, David Philip, coll. « Global Issues », 2000.

NIANGORAN, Martial, « Changements climatiques à Korhogo. Protéger les bois sacrés en encourageant le reboisement », in *Fraternité Matin*, cahier *Environnement & développement durable*, 14 February 2013, p.20-21.

PICHLER, Renato, « Les Bishnoïs, une vie sans tuer », in *Vegi-Info*, avril 2000.

UNITED NATIONS ENVIRONMENT PROGRAM (UNEP), *Annual Report 2008*.

SACHS, Ignacy, *L'écodéveloppement : stratégies pour le XXIᵉ siècle*, Collection Alternatives économiques, Paris, éditions Syros, 1997.

SAINT-MARC, Philippe, « Protection de la nature », in *Encyclopædia Universalis*, 1982, vol. 13, p. 690.

SZÉKELY, Edmond B., *The Essene Way: Biogenic Living*, I.B.S Intl., 1981.

TOURÉ, Moussa « Protection des écosystèmes. Ces menaces qui pèsent sur la biodiversité ivoirienne », in *Fraternité Matin*, cahier *Environnement & développement durable*, 4 December 2014, p. 19-20.

TOURÉ, Moussa, « Émission des GES. Des réductions encore insignifiantes », in *Fraternité Matin*, n° 13002, 13 March 2008, p. 3.

TOURÉ, Moussa, « Protection de la biodiversité. Une crise écologique guette la Côte d'Ivoire », cahier *Économie & environnement*, n° 97, p. VIII, in *Fraternité Matin*, 15 May 2006.

WILSON, Edward O., *The Future of Life*, New York, Alfred A. Knopf (Random House Inc.).

WORLD WILDLIFE FUND, *Living Planet Report 2008*.

TABLE OF CONTENTS